Sometimes, the quietest moments hold the most profound stories.

Index

Introduction

There are moments in life that change us forever, even when we don't realize it at the time. We walk through days filled with fleeting conversations, unexpected encounters, and quiet moments that leave marks deeper than we can fathom. This book is a reflection of those moments, the unspoken bonds, the whispers of love, and the journey of understanding that all of us go through in the process of growing and loving.

Writing *Whispers of Love and Unspoken Bond* has been a journey of my own one where I explored my heart, my thoughts, and the emotions that often go unsaid. Through the pages that follow, I invite you into a world where words are not always enough, but they are all we have to convey what lies beyond the surface.

This story is not just about love, it's about the quiet connection between souls, the things we don't say but still feel, and the bond that transcends time and distance. It's about the parts of us that are hidden, sometimes even from ourselves, and the way we learn to make sense of it all.

I hope this book offers you something more than just a story. I hope it touches the spaces within you that are too often left unexplored. As you read, I ask that you remember that these pages are more than just words; they are whispers of what we all have inside of us: the need to be understood, the desire to be seen, and the hope to be loved.

Prologue

I never planned to fall in love.
Especially not like this quietly, without warning, and definitely not with someone I never even spoke to properly.

It didn't start with a text.
There was no dramatic
confession. Just a
glance. A silence.
A strange kind of comfort I wasn't expecting.

Looking back now, I don't know the exact moment it began. Maybe it was the way they looked at the world as if they were always somewhere else. Maybe it was the way their presence felt familiar, even when we were strangers.
Or maybe it wasn't a moment at all.
Maybe it was a slow buildup of stolen glances, of unspoken things, of "what ifs" that never turned into anything more.

I used to think love had to be
loud to be real. But this one...
This one was made of silence.
And somehow, that made it louder than anything
else.
This story isn't
perfect. It's
messy.
Unfinished.
And maybe it never had a real beginning or
a proper ending. But it happened.
And it mattered.

Even if no one else ever knew.

Chapter 1: The First Glance

I didn't notice them right away.

It was just another ordinary class, the kind where the ceiling fan spins lazily, conversations hum in the background, and everything feels a little too slow to matter. I sat there, half-listening, half-drifting.

And then

something shifted.

A pause. A

stillness.

The kind that makes you look up

without knowing why. And there they

were.

Not doing anything special. Just standing by the window, sunlight falling across their face as if it belonged there. Head tilted slightly. Eyes lost in some far-off thought. Calm. Quiet. Untouchable.

But present. So present, it felt

impossible to look away. I froze. No

words. No blink. Just silence.

It wasn't an attraction. Not yet.
It was sharp, sudden, impossible to ignore.

The kind of wondering that makes you ask: What do they think about when no one's watching? What would their smile look like if it wasn't guarded? What would their laughter sound like if it was real?

They didn't notice me. Or maybe they did, but didn't care. No spark. No connection. Just... stillness.

And maybe that was what made it stay.

Because in a world where everyone is desperate to be noticed, they seemed like someone who didn't need to be. And yet I noticed.

For the rest of the day, my thoughts drifted back to that window, that face, that silence. Like a dream slipping just out of reach.

Why did it feel like I already knew them?
Why did something shift inside me the

moment they looked away? I told myself it was

nothing. Just a passing glance.

But I was wrong.

Because the next day, I searched for them again. And the day after that. And before I realized it, I wasn't just glancing anymore I was waiting.

That was the beginning.
The first quiet thread in a story I never saw coming.

And if I had known how that single glance would turn into sparks, how it would change the way I understood silence, and how it would reshape the way I carried love, maybe I would have looked away.

But I didn't.
And that's why everything began to spark.

Chapter 2: When Eyes Begin to Speak

Some things don't need a beginning.
They just unfold quietly, like a page turning on its own.

We didn't meet through friends.
We didn't bump into each other holding books or coffee cups. There was no meet-cute moment the movies obsess over.

There was just... presence.

A few days after that first glance, I noticed something.
They always sat near the same window. Not too far, not too close. Like they existed in the background of every room silent, but never invisible. Their eyes moved like they were listening to thoughts louder than the noise around them.
And then it

happened.

They looked at

me.

This time not by

accident. And I

froze.

It wasn't the kind of stare that demanded attention. It wasn't intense.
But it was *real.*
Like they saw something behind me, or maybe *in* me I still don't know.

That glance lasted just long enough to
make me feel it. That spark. That
whisper.
That *maybe*.
And for the first time, I couldn't
look away. Days passed.
We didn't
speak. But
our eyes did.

Little moments
They'd glance at me mid-conversation with someone
else
I'd look up just in time to see them
already looking. No smiles. No waves.
Just... something.

A kind of unspoken bond.
The kind that forms without trying.
The kind you don't even realize you're building

until it's already there. And slowly, I started

noticing the details.

How they tucked their hair behind their ear
when they were nervous. How they tapped their
pen three times when lost in thought.
How they'd stare at the sky like it held answers they were too scared to ask.

And every day, I found a new reason to look forward to *just existing in the same space as them.*

It was
innocent.
Sweet.
But dangerous in the softest way.

Because nothing had been said, and yet... It felt like
we were speaking all the time.

We created a
rhythm, a
language of
silence.
Where glances became conversations, and moments
become memories before they even end.

And one day I swear it lasted only
three seconds. They smiled at me.

Just a little.
But enough to feel like the ground beneath me had shifted.
No one else
noticed. But I
did.

Because I'd been waiting for that moment without even realizing it.

That smile didn't

say "hi." It said
"I know."

And that's when I realized this wasn't
just something in my head.

Something was growing
between us. Something too
fragile to name, but too real
to ignore.

We still hadn't spoken.
But somehow... it already felt like we had shared a thousand things.

The glances were longer now.
The silences were heavier like they were
holding something. And the way we both
looked away at the exact same time? Like
two people scared of what would happen
if they didn't.

I don't remember how many days
passed like that. Maybe a week.
Maybe more.
But I remember every second of those silent exchanges

I started walking slower past the
places I'd see them. Started sitting
closer.
Started caring about things I didn't even notice before.

It's strange, isn't it?
How someone can become part of your world
without
ever saying a single word. But that's what happened.

And even though we hadn't spoken our eyes had already started a story that neither of us knew how to stop.

Chapter 3: A Voice in the Silence

Some silences are loud.
But the ones we shared? They were soft,
gentle, almost sacred. And maybe that's why I
was afraid to break them.

We had become so used to *not*
speaking, so familiar with the language
of eyes and half-smiles, that I feared
what words might do.
Would they ruin it? Or would they finally set it free?
It happened on a day that felt like nothing special.
Cloudy sky.
Warm air.
One of those afternoons that stretches lazily, like it has nowhere to
be.
I was alone sitting under that same tree we always passed.
The one that caught just enough light to
feel
golden around noon. And then, I saw them.

Not across the
room. Not
behind a
crowd.
They were walking

toward me. Not

quickly. Not slowly.

Just... deliberately.

My heart began to race in a way it
hadn't before. This wasn't a glance.

This wasn't a

coincidence. This

was *real.*

They stopped a few feet away and gave the softest, most nervous smile the kind that almost asked for permission to exist.

"Hi," they said.

Just that. One word. But it echoed through me like thunder.

I blinked, trying to remember how
breathing worked. "Hey," I replied,
barely above a whisper.

And suddenly, the air felt different.

We stood there for a moment, caught
in a new silence not the kind we were
used to, but a silence that was
waiting.

"I always see you around," they said.
Their voice was calm but unsure, like they didn't know
how this worked either. "I guess... I just never said
anything."

I smiled. "Yeah. Same here."

They sat down next to me, but
not too close. The perfect
distance like always.
We talked about

nothing. The

weather.

The books we never finished.
The way that one teacher always
mispronounced our names. And slowly...
the walls we never knew we built began to
fall.

Their voices became familiar.
Their laughter started filling
up the quiet. And for the first
time,

our silence wasn't what connected us anymore.

It was this space we were creating

together, word by word. "I thought you

hated me," they said suddenly.

"What?" I laughed. "I thought *you*

were ignoring me." They looked at

me, head tilted. "Why would I ignore

you?"

I shrugged, a little embarrassed. "I don't know. You just... seemed like someone who doesn't let people in easily."

They were quiet for a second. Then, with a softness that

almost broke me, they said "Neither do you."

And just like that... we understood each other even more.

The conversation didn't
last hours. We didn't
pour our hearts out.
But something shifted that day.

We had crossed a line not in a bad way, but
like finally opening a letter you'd been

too scared to read. And what we found inside

was... us.

Two people,
with too many
thoughts, too
much silence,
and just enough courage to speak anyway.

As they stood up to leave, they

turned and smiled "I'll see you

around?"

And this time,
My reply wasn't shy or hesitant.

"Yeah," I said, with a smile that finally *meant something.*
"I'll be here."

We had spoken.
The silence was broken.
And now, there was no going back.

What we had before was
beautiful. But this?
This was *becoming* something.

And I couldn't wait to find out what came next.

Chapter 4: Whispers on the Windowpane

The classroom buzzed with the faint rustle of notebooks, chalk against the board, and the dull voice of the math teacher echoing like background noise in a dream I wasn't part of. I sat three benches from the window, yet it felt like I was closer to the sky than the ground.

Math has always been numbers and formulas. But today, none of it made sense not because it was hard, but because something more complicated sat two benches away, wrapped in a quiet presence I couldn't ignore.

She was scribbling something in her notebook. Not class

notes. I knew that much. I turned to the window.

Outside, the sky was turning grey, not the stormy kind, but the soft, emotional kind, like it wanted to cry but was holding back.

I stared.

Not at the trees. Not at the rain stains forming on the old building walls. I stared because I was thinking of her. And how something about her felt like a memory I hadn't lived yet.

And just like that...
She looked up.
And her eyes met mine.

Not a second longer than
it had to. But long
enough.

Long enough for the air to feel different like we both knew the world was still moving, but this moment was standing still.

I looked away
first. She
smiled a
second.

Later that day, it rained.

Not heavily. Just enough to make everything smell like old textbooks and wet leaves.

We both stayed behind, waiting for the rain to settle. Coincidence, maybe. Fate, maybe more.

There was an old stone bench near the cycle stand, half-covered by the overhang. I sat. She walked over, holding her notebook like a shield.

"You look bored in math," she said suddenly, her voice a little unsure, like she was surprising even herself by talking.

I smirked. "Is it that obvious?"

She laughed. And in that laugh, something opened up like two strangers were no longer strangers.

She sat down

beside me. Not too

close. Not too far.

We talked about how boring the class was, how the teacher always wore the same color shirt, and how the window made it easier to survive it all.
That night, it

started. A

message.

Just
one.
From
her.

“Today’s rain made everything feel like a movie scene. You write poetry?”
I stared at the
screen. Then
typed:
“Only when the windowpane whispers.”
Typing
... She
replie
d:
“Then write me something when it rains again.”

We didn’t say much.
But that silence carried more than any
poem.
And that’s how it began not with fireworks, not with music
but with math classes, rain, awkward jokes,

and shared silence. That night, I sat in bed,

staring at her last message.

And for the first time in a long time, I felt it.
This wasn't just a passing moment.
It was
something.
Something soft.
Something real.

Something I didn't
understand but I
wanted more of it.

Chapter 5: The Bench We Never Left

The next day, I passed by that same bench again, the one half-soaked by yesterday's rain, half-shielded by the rusted tin shade near the cycle stand.

Empty.

But it still felt full.

As if our laughter from yesterday hadn't left.
As if the soft echo of her voice still lingered in the space between the raindrops and the stone.

I didn't sit.
I didn't need to.
Because somehow, I was still there.

In school, the math class returned the same chalk, same shirt, same tired expressions across the room. But for the first time, **I wasn't counting minutes.**
I was counting

glances. She

looked up at me.

I looked away.
And then she didn't.

She stared a second
longer. Hold it.
Dared me to

smile. And I

did.

It was strange how someone could walk into your life so quietly and yet, rearrange all the noise inside you.
Later that week, we ended up at that

bench again. Same place. Same seat.

Different from us.

There was no rain this time.
Just the sound of wind brushing through trees, and our conversation filling the rest of the silence.
We talked about everything about how she loved the smell of books but hated reading them, about how I pretended to be bored in class just to look out the window, about dreams that felt too far away, and fears that felt too close.

We laughed at things that weren't even funny.
Because it wasn't about the joke it was about the *excuse*

to smile at each other. A week passed.

Then two.

The bench became ours not because we claimed it, but because no one else ever sat there. As if the world itself knew that place belonged to something that hadn't been spoken out loud.

We never said
"let's meet
there." But we
did.

After school.
Before
tuition.
During the short breaks where nothing really happened but we

remembered them anyway. She started bringing small snacks. I

started remembering her favorite ones.

Sometimes, we'd talk about nothing.
Other times, we'd fall silent and that was okay too.

Because in that silence, she'd sit with her hair gently swaying in the wind, and I'd sit with a heart slowly learning how to listen.

One evening, when the sky was melting into pink and gold, and the breeze carried the smell of wet earth and faraway flowers, she whispered:

"This bench... it's becoming my favorite part of the day."

I didn't say
anything. But
I nodded.

Because I didn't want to break that moment with words.

It's funny how some places don't
belong on maps, but they still hold
the biggest parts of your heart.

It's funny how some places don't
belong on maps, but they still hold
the biggest parts of your heart.

And that old bench?
It wasn't just wood and stone anymore.
It was the start of something that felt infinite in a very fleeting world.
A place we never planned to
make ours. But somehow...

The bench we never left.

Chapter 6: Rain Between Us

Some days stay with you forever not because they were planned, but because they weren't.

It had been a humid afternoon, the kind that makes everything feel heavier than it should. The school day had crawled, the final bell rang with a strange relief, and students spilled into the streets like water finally released from a dam.

She and I had been walking a little slower than usual.

It was never official, but somehow, walking her halfway home had become a silent ritual. We didn't talk about it. It just happened. Every day. Sometimes we talked about nonsense.
Sometimes, nothing at all. But it never felt forced. It felt... like something we didn't want to break.

That day, the sky looked like it was holding back tears.

"I think it's going to rain," she said, tilting her head upward, smiling as if the clouds were old friends she'd missed.

"You say that like it's a good thing," I

replied, shielding my eyes. She laughed. "It

is. I love the rain."

A few minutes later, the clouds opened. Not a light drizzle. A downpour. Sudden and honest — the kind that soaks you in seconds, washing away everything but the moment itself.

People rushed under trees, closed their umbrellas late, pulled out their phones to save them from water damage.

But she? She stood there.

Arms half-spread. Hair slowly plastered to her

skin. Eyes closed. Smiling. I stood frozen. Half

in awe. Half unsure.

"You coming or what?" she yelled over the rain, waving me into a small tea stall nearby with faded yellow tin roofing and the smell of chai and wet earth mixing perfectly.

We stood there. Dripping. Breathing. Laughing.

An old film song was playing from the shopkeeper's ancient radio, something about love and monsoons and stolen glances. It was almost too perfect to be real.

"You really like the rain that much?" I asked, wringing out my shirt. "I don't just like it. I wait for it," she said, looking out at the world now blurred in water and wind. "It makes everything feel slower. Softer. Like time pauses for people like us."

"People like us?" I asked, raising an eyebrow.

She shrugged. "People who don't say

things out loud." Silence.

The good kind.
The kind that says everything before you even ask.

She took out a chocolate from her pocket that melted a little and broke it in two. "You want half?"

And just like that, under a leaky roof, beside a boiling kettle and a puddle forming at our feet it felt like we weren't two people anymore.

It felt like one shared pause in a world that never stopped moving.

I looked at her really and in that single glance, I knew. Whatever this was between us, it had taken root. Quietly. Softly. Like rain soaking into dry soil.

I wanted the moment to last longer, but the clouds were already beginning to move. The sun peeked out like it was embarrassed by what it had seen.

She looked up. "Let's walk a little. I don't

mind being wet." Neither did I.

We walked. No umbrella. No hurry. Just stories.
And laughter. And silence that felt like music.

And somewhere between two puddles and the wind tangling her hair she said something that made my heart stop.

"You make the rain feel warmer."

I didn't say anything back. Because sometimes, saying nothing is the most honest answer.

That night, I typed a message and left it in drafts:

"I think today... something began between us. Maybe quietly. But it began."

I never sent it.
But she must've felt it too.

Because the next morning, she was waiting for me at the same spot, same soft smile, like the rain had left something behind.

Not just wet shoes and

muddy roads. But

something more.

Something only we could see.

Something between us.

Chapter 7: Vacations Without You

It was only a few days after that rain-drenched walk home that the school halls went silent. Winter break was announced with a two-week pause from the uniforms, the benches, the chalk dust, the windows... and from her.

I should've been happy. Everyone was. Freedom from assignments, no early mornings, and a whole lot of lazy afternoons ahead. But instead, it hit me unexpectedly this time, I'd be free of everything... except the thought of her.

"Hey, vacation's coming," she said, grinning that day. "Winter is my favorite."

I remember that smile vividly. It wasn't just about the holidays. Her eyes sparkled in a way that told stories of soft shawls, of hot chocolate, of tiny paperbacks half-read under a blanket, of nights spent watching the stars in silence.
I wanted to be a part of that world even if only through a screen.

The first few days were quiet. I'd open my phone,
close it, open it again. Should I text first? Is she
busy? Would it be weird?
And then a simple *"Hey"* from her. Just that. But enough to make the whole room warmer than the heater ever could.

We talked late into the night. Not every night, not always long. But each message felt like a thread holding us together. We talked about movies, her winter playlist (yes, she had one), how she loved the way the cold air made everything feel slower and quieter. She sent me a photo of her garden all dew and pale light and said,

"Mornings like this make me write poems I never finish."
I didn't say it, but I wished I could be the poem she'd never want to stop writing.

But texts are tricky. Sometimes you wait. Sometimes she replies late. Sometimes you wonder if she's lost interest or just fell asleep with the phone in her hand. And each second of silence stretches longer than it should.

I started noticing things more: the empty streets outside, the misty glass of my window, the way I'd type a message and delete it five times before sending. She occupied everything, even in her absence.

My friends didn't get it.
"Chill, it's just a break."
But how do I explain to someone that this wasn't just a break?

Winter was her season. But somehow, it began to feel like mine too. Every memory of her started glowing under the pale sun. That red sweater she wore once, the way her voice sounded softer when the wind blew, how her fingers always played with the end of her sleeves while thinking. It was funny how I remembered things I never consciously noticed before.

I wrote about her. Not poems. Just fragments. Sentences half-formed. Thoughts unfinished.

"There's a kind of silence that echoes more when the person you miss isn't loud to begin with." "She didn't leave, but she wasn't there either, not in the way I needed."
"Winter makes it easier to pretend you're not crying, it's just cold."

As the vacation neared its end, the excitement that usually came with going back to school was replaced with anxiety. What would change? Would she still talk to me the same way? Would the classroom feel the same? Would we sit on that bench again?

But one night, just before school was to reopen, she texted:
"Let's meet before school reopens. Maybe near the café?"

My fingers shook. Not from the cold. But from a warmth

that suddenly rushed in. She missed me too. Maybe not

as much. Maybe not the same way. But enough.

And in that moment, I realized vacations without her weren't empty... they were filled with everything I didn't know I felt. Not just a gap in routine. But a space she unknowingly filled with memories, with longing, with hope.

Chapter 8: Your Name in My Silence

They say silence speaks volumes, but what they never tell you is how heavy it feels when you're carrying a name inside it.

The school reopened with the same bell, the same dusty corridors, and the same wooden benches. Yet something had changed not outside, but inside me. I saw her again on that first day, her hair tied a little higher, her bag slung over one shoulder, and that same sparkle still living in her eyes. She smiled, and I forgot how to breathe. I wanted to say something, maybe a "Hey, missed you," or a casual "How were your holidays?" But the words tangled somewhere between my heart and my throat. So, I just smiled back and said nothing.

Math class returned to its boring rhythm, but the window became something new. I wasn't staring outside anymore I was staring at her reflection in the glass. Sometimes she'd glance my way, and I'd quickly look away, pretending to be lost in numbers. But I wasn't. I was counting the things I never said.
One... I missed you.
Two... I thought about you
every night. Three... I saved
your goodnight texts. Four...
I'm falling for you.
But I never reached five, because five meant saying it out loud.

We still chatted, but less than before. Shorter replies. Longer delays. Emoji answers where words once lived. Something in me panicked. I reread our old messages like pages from a story I couldn't let end. I kept checking if she was online, and every time I typed "Hey," I backspaced it until the screen went blank again. Strange how someone could be so close, yet suddenly feel so far.

One afternoon in class, she passed me a note. A doodle of a star, and beneath it: *Some things are better left unsaid.*
I stared at it too long, trying to decide if she was talking about us.

That night, I lay on my bed staring at the ceiling, phone in hand, wondering why silence suddenly felt safer than honesty. Maybe I was afraid of losing the comfort we had. Maybe saying it out loud would shatter the fragile thing we were slowly building. Or maybe I already knew the answer, and just didn't want to hear it. I wrote her name in the corner of my notebook, then again, and again, until the page became a quiet scream I couldn't voice.

She had become a habit, one that lived between my breaths and beat between my pauses. She wasn't just someone I liked anymore. She was someone I carried. In songs. In empty benches. In missed glances. In every silent moment I didn't fill with her name.

And yet, I stayed silent. Because love, especially the quiet kind, isn't always about confessions. Sometimes it's about cherishing what you have, even if you never get to call it yours.

Sometimes it's enough just to sit beside someone, knowing they

I don't know. And maybe... never will.

Chapter 9: The Farewell You Do Not Know Was One

The last exam day didn't feel like "the last." It felt like just another day. That's how real goodbyes often arrive quietly, like guests who don't ring the doorbell.

She was standing a few steps ahead of the gate, fixing her scarf as the winter wind played gently with her hair. The cold sunlight wrapped around everything like a soft filter, nothing too bright, nothing too heavy. Just... enough.

I held the small gift in my hand not wrapped too perfectly, but from the heart. It wasn't anything fancy, just a token. Maybe a memory disguised as an object.

I thought I'd ask for a photo. Just one. Something to hold on to. But my voice couldn't find its way out of my throat. Maybe because somewhere, deep down, I knew... that this wasn't just the end of exams. It was the end of a chapter we didn't even know we were writing.

She smiled at me with that quiet smile.

"So... it's done." "Yeah... done." I

replied, but I didn't mean the exam.

We walked a little. She was going her way; I was going mine. Two paths, two homes. But that walk felt like a thread being pulled from something soft and delicate like an old sweater coming undone, one loop at a time.

"Hey," I said, stopping. She turned, curious. I stretched out my hand with the gift. "This is... just something. For you."

She looked at it, then at me. Her smile didn't widen, but her eyes softened. She took it like it was something fragile, something she'd remember, even if she wouldn't say so.

And then... she walked away.

No dramatic pause. No hug. No second glance. Just like any other walk home.

But I stood there, watching her figure fade slowly with every step. I thought the world would pause for a moment, that the sky would change color, that the wind would whisper, *"This is it."* But nothing happened.

Except the ache.

Not the heavy, screaming kind but the quiet kind. The kind that nests inside you, builds a home, and whispers in moments you least expect.

That night, I didn't sleep.
I didn't even open the gift box I had left for her. I didn't ask if she liked it. I didn't check if she went home safely. I didn't send a goodbye message.

Because how do you say goodbye... to something that never officially started?

It was a farewell written in invisible ink. A goodbye wrapped in silence. A closing chapter with no title... just this vague, lingering echo.

She didn't know it was

the last. Maybe I didn't

either.

But somewhere between our final glance and that cold winter wind, the story paused. I just paused.

Forever on that one page.

Chapter 10: The Unspoken Bond

It had been weeks.

Vacations melted into routine. Routine into silence. And silence... into memory.

I didn't delete the chats. I didn't mute her status updates. I didn't stop myself from typing something... and then backspacing it before pressing send. I just let things *be.*

It wasn't far. It wasn't ego. It wasn't even about moving on.

It was that quiet bond, the kind that doesn't ask for attention. The kind that survives in small echoes. In my favorite song. A quote on a stranger's story. A scarf that looked like hers. A laugh that sounded almost like the one I knew by heart.

And somewhere in that

stillness, I realized... We never

really said anything, did we?

No confessions. No "I like you." No promises. No what-ifs. But somehow, it *was there*. Unwritten.

Unspoken. Undeniable. She must've felt it

too.

I remember one night, it was past midnight. She uploaded a photo of just a blurry city street under yellow lights. No caption. Just that.

But somehow... It said everything. That she missed something too. Even if we weren't talking, some parts of our stories were still whispering to each other quietly, like best friends who never really stopped being best friends even if they grew distant.

The unspoken bond wasn't about
what we said. It was about what
we never needed to say.

Like that one time I almost bumped into her in a bookstore aisle. We both froze. She laughed softly, tucked her hair behind her ear the exact same way she used to and said, "Still walking like you own the place, huh?"

And I said, "Still showing up in the places I

thought were mine." We laughed. But we

both knew... that laughter had layers.

We didn't ask how life was. We didn't ask if
things were okay. Because we already knew:
we were okay, just... separately now.

But the bond?
It was still there like a song that plays in the background
when everything else goes quiet.

Like a bookmark in an
old book. Like a bench
no one sat on after us.

Like a memory that didn't grow old just

faded into sepia. We were never lovers.

We were never just
friends. We were
something else.
Something rare.

A quiet, beautiful bond that never needed a name.

Maybe in another life, we would've said the things we couldn't.
Maybe in another life, we wouldn't be afraid to ruin the

magic by speaking it out loud. But in this life...

We loved silently.
And lost... just the same.

Chapter 11: In Another Life, Maybe

Sometimes, I wonder if we had been someone else in another life. A version of ourselves where we weren't bound by time, by distance, or by the limits we put on each other. Where love wasn't something we tiptoed around but something we gave freely, without fear.

If I think hard enough, I can picture it. We're in another life. A place where the sun doesn't set before we've said everything we needed to say, where we laugh without feeling the ache of what might've been.

In this life, things had ended quietly. No grand gestures. No dramatic goodbyes. Just that silence, the one that stretched between us like a gap I couldn't bridge.

But in another life, maybe it would've been different.

Maybe we'd be walking side by side, no distance, no hesitation. Maybe our hands would brush accidentally, and it wouldn't feel like an accident at all. It would feel like it was always meant to be, like every second we spent apart had led us here. Maybe our love would have been simple then. Maybe it wouldn't have taken years to grow.

I'd ask about your day, and you'd ask about mine. And for once, the answer wouldn't be a lie. Maybe we wouldn't have said "I'm fine" when everything felt wrong. Maybe in this other life, we would've let each other in, really in, without the fear of getting hurt.

I can almost hear your voice, clear and calm, without the silence that always followed. The words that we never said would be spoken here. Not in the way we held back in the past. But in a way that felt natural, like breathing.

In another life, maybe we wouldn't have needed to leave things unsaid. We could've kissed goodbye, walked out the door together, and felt our hearts beat in sync. We could've been happy. We could've been the way I always dreamed we would be.

But the truth is, this life isn't that life.

This life is full of "maybe"s. And "what if"s.

And as much as I want to believe in that other life, I know that this one we're living now is the only one we get. The moments we didn't share, the words we didn't say... they make up the beautiful, painful story of who we were.

Maybe, in the next life, we'll get another chance. Maybe we'll get it right. Maybe the stars will align, and we won't be too scared, too lost, too busy to love the way we were meant to.

But until then...
I'll keep our story in my heart, the one that's quiet and unspoken, the one that will forever live in the spaces between the words we never said.

And in this life, that will have to be enough.

Chapter 12: Whispers of Love

In the quietest corners of the heart, there exists a space where words fall silent. It is here, in this sacred silence, that love whispers its softest truths. The kind of love that does not need to shout, does not need to demand; it is the love that simply is. The kind of love that lingers, invisible to the world, but felt by those who know its touch.

And it is here, in this space, that our story ends not with grand gestures or endings neatly tied in ribbons, but with the soft, delicate sound of a heart that will never forget. The whispers of love, faint but eternal, like a melody played only for those who choose to listen.

In the end, it wasn't the moments we spent together that defined us. No, it was everything we never said, the conversations that danced around us but never touched the surface, the looks we shared that spoke volumes but were left unexplained. It was the quiet knowing that we had something powerful, something unbreakable, yet something we couldn't fully hold onto.

I've learned that love isn't always about the loud, dramatic confessions or the perfect timing. Sometimes, it's the things that remain unsaid that carry the most weight. It's the softest touches, the lingering glances, the way our souls reach out to each other in the quietest of moments.

Whispers of love are not shouted into the world. They are felt in the spaces between, in the quiet of the night, in the gentle brush of a hand or the shared silence between two hearts that understand more than words ever could.

Sometimes, I wonder if you hear these whispers that echo between us, the ones I never had the courage to say. But you must hear them, because every time I close my eyes, I see you. I hear you. I feel you. And in this unspoken bond, we are forever connected.

Perhaps love, true love, is meant to be felt more than spoken.

Perhaps it is the quiet that makes it beautiful, the way it lingers in the air, undisturbed by the noise of the world. It's in the spaces we shared, the memories that float like fragile wisps of smoke, untouchable and ever present.

And maybe, just maybe, love isn't meant to be understood. Maybe it is only meant to be lived, breathed, felt, and never fully explained. It is a story without a beginning or an end. It is a story that exists outside of time, slipping through the cracks of reality, never fully anchored to this world.

We were never meant to have closure, I suppose. That's the beauty of it. The love we shared was never something I could fully capture in words, and maybe I never will. But I'll carry it with me, always, in the whispers that follow me through the quiet moments of my life.

Somewhere, deep in my heart, I still hear it. A soft, tender whisper that says, *"I loved you, and I always will."*

And perhaps that is the greatest love of all, the one that is silent but eternal, the one that never demands to be seen but is felt in every heartbeat, in every moment that passes, in every second we spend apart yet forever bound together by the unspoken.

"Love is not bound by time or space. It is not confined to the words we speak or the promises we make. It lives in the silent echoes, in the whispers we hear when no one else is listening."

The Final Letter

The words that I never said to you, the things I never had the courage to voice, have now found their way into this letter. It's strange, isn't it? How something as simple as paper and ink can hold so much more than just words it holds pieces of the heart, fragments of a time when I was too afraid to speak, too hesitant to let my feelings out into the world.

This is the letter I should have written years ago, but it didn't come then. And maybe that's okay. Maybe it wasn't supposed to come until now. We both walked away, and the distance only made me realize how deeply I cared, how much I had kept hidden beneath the surface. I couldn't say it then, but I can say it now, through this letter.

I still remember your smile, the way you would laugh without restraint, the way your eyes sparkled when you talked about things you loved. Those memories have stayed with me, like a soft, quiet hum in the background of everything I've done since then. They've shaped me, even if you didn't know it. Even if I never told you.

I don't know if this letter will ever reach you. Maybe it's only for me. Maybe it's for you, wherever you are, in whichever corner of the world you've wandered to. But I want you to know that I don't regret anything. Not the moments we shared, not the things we left unsaid, and certainly not the bond that once held us together.

Life, with its winding roads and unexpected turns, might have taken us on separate paths, but you will always be a part of me. You always will be.

The unspoken bond, the whispers of love, they weren't meant to be shouted from the rooftops. They lived quietly, gently, between us. And that's enough.

I hope that wherever you are, you're happy. I hope you've found peace in your own way, just as I've found mine. This is my final letter to you, not because I don't have more to say, but because I've said everything I need to, and sometimes, silence is the loudest message we can send.

So, here it is the last word, the final goodbye, wrapped in the quiet of everything we shared. Take care.

A Letter to Myself

Dear Me,

It's strange, really, to sit down and write this letter to myself, the person I've known all my life but still sometimes fail to truly understand. I've often wondered what you'd say to me if you could speak out loud, and so I write this as an answer to that silent question.

The days of confusion, doubt, and unspoken moments may seem distant now, but they were never a burden. Instead, they were the silent teachers that shaped us into who we are today. Every struggle, every unanswered call, every conversation that could never be finished they were all part of a larger story unfolding.

I've watched you carry the weight of expectations, sometimes pushing so hard that you forget to breathe. But in those moments, you've learned. You've learned what matters most, and you've learned to trust your journey, no matter how uncertain it may seem.

There were days you wanted to give up, days when you thought your heart might break under the weight of the world. Yet, here we are standing stronger. You've held on. You've kept moving forward with quiet resilience, and that matters more than any grand achievement could ever.

I see you, with your eyes full of dreams, searching for meaning in every corner of your world. You've found beauty in places most people overlook, and in doing so, you've given meaning to the smallest, most fleeting moments. Whether it was an accidental glance, a shared laugh, or the quiet of a rainy afternoon, you've learned to savor it all.

But I also see the sadness that lingers in you, like a song you can't quite forget. You've been afraid to face it, afraid to acknowledge how deeply it runs. Yet in silence, I want you to know that there is no shame in carrying this grief. It is simply part of you.

So, I ask you, with all the tenderness I've learned to give myself, don't be so hard on us. We've made mistakes, and we've faltered, but we've also grown. And as we stand here, looking ahead, I ask you to remember one thing: You are enough. You are always enough.

There is no perfect roadmap, no guidebook that tells you exactly how to live. But the way you've walked, through every storm, and under every star, has been your own. And that, my friend, is the only thing that matters.

So, don't rush. Don't wish away the days. Life is already unfolding, beautiful and wild in its own right. Trust it. Trust us.

Thank you for never giving up. Thank you for being brave enough to write this story, to feel this deeply, and to keep moving forward, no matter the direction.

With every ounce of love,
Me

About the Author

Jay Kumar Gurung, an aspiring entrepreneur and storyteller, is passionate about blending real-life experiences with creative expression. At just 17, his journey is shaped by introspection, personal growth, and a quiet curiosity about the world around him.

His debut book, *Whispers of Love and Unspoken Bond*, explores the delicate threads of connection, love, and the silences that often say the most. Drawing from the moments that linger the ones left unsaid, the ones that changed everything Jay writes not only to express but to connect.

He believes in the quiet strength of stories how they heal, inspire, and reveal hidden parts of ourselves. As he builds his future, this book stands as a gentle step forward not just into writing, but into the world he's slowly shaping with sincerity and courage.

Acknowledgments

This book wouldn't have come to life without the unwavering support of those who have been part of my journey in ways big and small.

To my family, whose love and belief in me have been my steady anchor. You've given me the courage to follow my dreams and to see beauty in every step, no matter how uncertain. Your sacrifices are the foundation of every word written here.

To my friends, who've shared in the quiet moments and loud laughter, for reminding me of the importance of connection. Your perspectives have shaped my own, and your encouragement has been a constant source of inspiration.

To every reader who picks up this book, thank you for allowing me to share a piece of my heart with you. It is you who breathe life into these words, and for that, I am forever grateful.

And finally, to the quiet spaces in between the noise, where my thoughts took shape for they have allowed me to craft something that is more than just a story. It is a reflection of everything I have learned, and everything I still have yet to understand.

Thank you.

www.ingramcontent.com/pod-product-compliance
Lightning Source LLC
Chambersburg PA
CBHW050025170726
48282CB00025B/557
* 9 7 8 9 3 3 4 4 0 8 4 9 2 *